HANS
IS
DEAD

ALSO BY BRIAN BARTON

HANS

IS

DEAD

BRIAN

BARTON

For J.Y.

MY FLYING DREAM IS ODD given my fear of flying. I soar high into the clouds and turn on my cloaking device until it flickers like a fluorescent bulb around my form. Now I'm invisible. It's peaceful up here in these blue, blue skies because there's no darkness, no pain, no demons that can't be controlled.

The dream is one thing but I've also gained a new interest: jets. Maybe my hobby is a vestige of my teenage love of sports cars but I can't get enough of fast planes. Give me commercial jets, military aircraft, and private jets on the ground or in the skies and watch me gawk like a child. But my interest in aviation strikes anyone that knows me as odd—especially given my fear.

My fear of flying shadowed me like a dark cloud from adolescence into adulthood. It was worse than anything I'd experienced before or since. I'm talking about physical and psychological symptoms that were off the charts: stabbing chest pain, difficulty breathing, heart palpitations, sweating, and paranoia. Whenever I flew I felt like I was inhaling oxygen by the thimbleful.

The shaking and crying were the worst of it because they were impossible to mask. I got used to crying in front of strangers and apologizing afterwards. But I never did shake the shame.

My anxiety would surface days before a flight and wouldn't abate until I was back at home in my own bed. I was apoplectic before takeoffs and landings, and cried during turbulence like a toddler dropped off on the first day of school.

Family and friends spoke to me in gentle tones about their own strategies for alleviating flight phobia in an effort to help. They sent me articles from experts with impressive credentials and a litany of overlapping advice: positive visualization, desensitization, exposure therapy, Tai Chi, E.M.D.R., hypnosis, and cognitive behavioral therapy. I tried it all, even adding psychotherapy and medication to the mix to make sure I wasn't missing anything. None of it helped. Though I really did enjoy the Tai Chi.

One doctor prescribed a drug so powerful that I arrived at LAX a slurry mess. I stumbled out of the jetway and grabbed a wall like a frat boy after a bender. I couldn't even make it to the rental car counter, and thank god. I only made it to my hotel with assistance.

I lost at least a half dozen promotions due to my fear of flying and was fired from two jobs because of it. The fear also saddled every romantic relationship I had. Not surprisingly, women don't enjoy taking care of men on vacation. My ex-girlfriends weren't unsympathetic to my needs but they hadn't exactly signed up for therapist duty and I didn't blame them.

But then a few years ago something miraculous happened. My fear of flying vanished as mysteriously as it had arrived. I was so grateful that I began a love affair with the skies.

Nowadays, I love to fly. I'll even battle a coworker for dibs on a business trip. It's not for the career benefits or air miles. And it's not for the shopping, boozing, or schmoozing at the destination. I don't care if it's Missouri or Milan because I'm not interested in history, fashion, architecture, food, museums, or music. I don't care about social media bragging rights or making my Facebook friends jealous. All I want to do is float on the clouds six miles high.

These days I'm busy watching planes because their sound and form fire my lust like an adolescent with a schoolgirl crush. A jet roars overhead and it's like a call to arms. Suddenly I'm primed for the hunt or ready to kill for the U-S-of-A. It's a scorched earth scenario with all guns blazing and where only one man walks away. *U-S-A! U-S-A! U-S-A!*

A KLM 777 I saw earlier in the year at SFO really did a number on me. Her cerulean blue hull caught a glint of California sunlight just as I was walking through the terminal and it stopped me mid-step. She was covered in a sweeping graphic design that alternated between KLM colors and unpainted aluminum that shone like chrome.

She looked like the jewel she was against the pale blue sky and gray tarmac and I was awestruck—such majesty of beauty and function. It took everything in my power not to lollygag at the window and press my nose to the glass. I wanted to devour her supple curves, aerodynamic engine cowls, turbine fan blades, and aluminum skin. She welcomed my every overture and I still wanted to linger on her form.

Sometimes I'll catch myself geeking out over commercial jets and comparing the latest models. I'll find the newest planes at my favorite carriers and compare them side by side, like a pair of Pokémon character cards. How far do they fly and how fast? Which one can make the furthest nonstop flight and how much does it cost for a first class ticket leaving tomorrow?

It would be wrong to talk about planes and not mention "the boys" because they're the reason I have my beloved jets. The Wright Brothers made their first powered, manned flight in 1903, but their journey outshone their invention. The boys were imbued with an optimism and curiosity that was rare.

In fact, Wilbur and Orville enjoyed many avocations before they launched the age of aviation. They loved bicycles, birds, books, engineering, printing, manufacturing, history, construction, retail, and architecture. Their curiosity knew no bounds.

Academy Award-winning Hollywood producer Brian Grazer says curiosity deserves to be cultivated in our schools and workplaces and that it merits more attention than its cousins "creativity" and "innovation." In *A Curious Mind: The Secret to a Bigger Life*, he even credits it for his own success. "Curiosity has been the most valuable quality, the most important resource, the central motivation of my life," he writes.

Take one look around and you can see that many of our most important discoveries were birthed from the minds of the curious. Alexander Graham Bell. Jonas Salk. Benjamin Franklin. Eli Whitney. Marie Curie. Who else but these curious souls could have discovered, respectively, the telephone, the polio vaccine, electricity, the cotton gin, and radioactivity? Who would fly a kite in an electrical storm except someone deeply curious (if a little bonkers)?

The Wrights changed the world on the wind-swept sand dunes of Kitty Hawk and Kill Devil Hills, but my real thanks goes to David

McCullough, who transported me there in his book *The Wright Brothers*. Reading it, I felt immersed in the early twentieth century as the boys traveled through North Carolina, Ohio, France, Germany, and places in between.

I stood inside the Wright's Dayton, Ohio bike shop as they built wind tunnels and machined parts for their planes. I watched Orville as he worked the metal lathe. I cheered from the sand dunes at Kill Devil Hills, North Carolina when the boys took flight, and I cursed their misfortunes. It was obvious the boys weren't in it for the fame because they didn't chase money or notoriety. They were driven instead by simple curiosity.

But my admiration for Wilbur and Orville is distant and sepia-toned. I see them in photos from 1910 looking handsome and trim in their suits and ties but there's something I can't understand. There they are again in photos flying over Kill Devil Hills and Huffman Prairie but I still can't compute what I see. They're flying hundreds of feet in the air on machines they built themselves? They were *bicycle mechanics*?

But if I look carefully at the photos sometimes I can catch a glimmer of that magic. They're aloft over landscapes as vast as oceans and I'll find myself taking an extra breath. I'll look at the vistas underneath their wings and barely be able to make out the homes on the horizon and I'll feel a sense of optimism. And it buoys my spirit. They're soaring high above it all and I'm dumbstruck because I'm in total awe.

DREAMING

I CAN'T PREDICT MY DREAM'S arrival or encourage its appearance. It only visits when it pleases and it doesn't like attention. But when it does materialize I'm grateful. It's a happy surprise, like arriving at work and learning your boss is out for the day.

Dinner and conversation are how I wrap up my evenings, then it's goodnights to the boy and maybe some fun for us. Then I'll crawl over to my side of the bed and grab a pillow before I relinquish control to the magic elf who runs the dream theater in my mind.

My flying dream always starts off the same way. I'm strolling down the sidewalks of Manhattan's East Village in the 1920s. Wearing a sharp suit and tie, I'm anachronistically singing an Eagles tune like *Tequila Sunrise* or *I Can't Tell You Why*. I feel hopeful and the feeling grows until I arrive at the corner of East 7th Street and First Avenue, where I begin rising in the air.

Maybe it's my mood that sets me aloft or maybe it's the smell of pickles from a nearby deli. Regardless, within moments I am airborne.

Soon I'm flying without fear, like a doughy Mary Poppins. I reverse direction and fall back to earth then spring off the sidewalk as if it were a trampoline and bounce back into the sky. Eventually the wind carries me to Brooklyn, right to Prospect Park. This is my favorite part of the dream because I have an epic view of springtime: frisbee players, families, kids playing in the sun. People are picnicking, talking, eating, drinking, sleeping, staring, and doing nothing at all. A few dogs and owners lope around the park's perimeter while couples canoodle in the shade.

A group of trees sit on a small hill. Their branches slough off hundreds of leaves in the breeze like a choreographed snowfall. The translucent green and yellow cascade flickers against the setting sun with each leaf floating to the ground fulfilling its short destiny.

Give me more beauty! I tell the magic elf who runs my dreams. *I want more!*

We have a shared purpose, the magic elf and I, because he wants to share the world's beauty and I want to enjoy it. I feel like the only person at a movie theater watching God's personal highlight reel. And the show is epic.

I spot a black teenager in a red shirt, racing down the sidewalk and laughing with his friends. He has a fade haircut and a smile that beams innocence. Trying to catch a basketball that's been ransomed by another member of his group, the teenager stops suddenly and looks up to where my figure floats in space.

"Mister! Mister! Show me!" he says.

I'm caught by a gust of wind and start floating away, so he takes off after me. His friends yell at him to stop but he ignores them and continues in pursuit. The breeze pushes me slowly across the park and he easily catches up until he's right underneath me. Now we're both moving along at a gentle clip and he's dodging park goers and the occasional stroller to keep up.

"Flying is easy!" I say. "Just do what I do. Now jump!"

He jumps but can't get off the ground. Then the wind blows harder and I'm spirited away. I yell back some words of encouragement and hope that he can hear.

I touch down on the street outside the park and hear someone running toward me. Bouncing back into the air I look down in time to see the boy arrive at the spot where I just landed, hunched over, hands on thighs, spent, looking up at the sky. Our eyes meet in a shared sadness—and I fly higher.

I realize I'm angry at this scripted adventure and I want off the ride. *Give me another dreamscape*, I beg the magic elf because now I feel stuck, like I'm on a theme park ride I want to end.

A few moments later I'm hovering over a small meadow, thirty feet in the air, motionless. I see a flash of red and hear someone walk through the grass before a figure appears below me. It's the boy. We see each other and he smiles.

"Show me! Show me!" he yells.

"I will. Just be patient, okay?" I say. "Just do exactly what I'm doing. Go ahead and try it again, because I think it's going to work."

And now I'm up. Eyes open.

GRIEVING

THE SIDE OF THE BED where my girlfriend sleeps is a heap of covers with several peaks. I examine the textile mountain like an intelligence officer with a satellite image of Tora Bora and try to decode its meaning. Finally, I poke the pile with my finger, looking for life. But she's gone.

I grab my phone and open Twitter and find a tweet from Don Henley, co-founder, drummer, and vocalist of Eagles. He's tweeting about his friend and band mate, Eagles' front man, vocalist, guitarist, and co-founder Glenn Frey. It's a love note of sorts and conveys Henley's warm feelings for Frey. I read this in my bleary morning state and think, "Why the fuck is Don Henley tweeting about Glenn Frey?"

A toilet flushes in the bathroom and the water is running. *She's in the shower already. Shit—I'm going to have to wait my turn. At least I have a little time before work.* I roll over on the bed in a tangle of covers and bring the phone to my face.

Writing about Frey online seems superfluous. How could you sum him up in 140 characters and why is Henley trying? Besides, social media is small and Frey is big, so a tweet seems like a gross disservice, like a one-word essay on Abraham Lincoln.*

My lips tighten because I'm angry at the brevity imposed by social media, and by our short attention spans. I'm sad that we no longer honor artists with sweeping narratives filled with nuance and emotion. This isn't what Frey needs at all. What Frey needs is a twelve-volume biography, a six-part mini-series, a dozen documentaries—*something.*

Then again *I* could be the problem. Maybe I'm to blame because I'm the erstwhile cultural critic who's quick to pass down judgments from atop his high horse. I'd like to blame this on the fact that I'm a writer and I've always preferred long stories to quick hits. Maybe that's why we writers rail against the Web's penchant for click-bait headlines, 100-word listicles, and animal attack videos.

I read stories because they immerse me in worlds I might otherwise not be able to inhabit. I read Anthony Bourdain because I want to know what it's like to eat raw seal carcass with Inuits in Quebec and not have to worry about getting blood on my slacks. I'll get lost in a Bourdain yarn about driving a perilous Vietnam highway because I'd rather not die from a fatal head-on.

So, please, don't tell me about Frey with a soundbite. Put me next to the Michigan boy in thrumming 1970s L.A. and show me his coming of age. Tell me about a man on a mission in the land of temptation, struggling to keep his nose clean and his head above water.

Give me a ringside seat to Frey's vices and virtues and his battles won and lost. Show me what artistic collaboration looks like when each player is at the top of their game and egos fade into the woodwork. Show me Frey shaking the hands of record execs over drinks at the Bel Air Hotel, then partying in the Hollywood Hills. I want to stand in the corner with Joni Mitchell, David Geffen, and Linda Rondstadt and hear them tell their tales, because I know you can't know a man without knowing his contemporaries. Give me Frey swimming laps in a Brentwood pool, then driving into the valley to chat with the disc jockeys and journalists who run that industry town.

Give me a story of promises made and broken, with me in the passenger seat and Frey at the wheel as we cruise above Mulholland with warm Santa Ana winds in our faces. I want to know what it's like to be at the top of the charts and at the bottom of the totem pole, still stuck in a shitty apartment and waiting for the first big check to clear.

I guess what I'm saying is that I want to know Frey because I want to understand the man behind the band who smoothed my adolescence. Eagles helped me on my journey growing up in Los Angeles and made me a lifelong fan from the moment my record player touched the vinyl of "Hotel California."

God knows, the band saw me through enough dark hours when I needed a friend. They watched me struggle but never judged, and I always got the feeling they wanted the best for me even when I didn't make the right choices. They gave me hope when I despaired and had my back when I thought all was lost. And they were there when I found my redemption.

Frey deserves our thanks for holding the band together through over forty years of tumultuous ups and downs. Through lineup changes, shifts in musical taste, the death of the record business, and the struggles in between. I don't care about the band's 150 million albums sold or their five number one hits because those metrics only mean something to the bean counters. Sales figures will never measure the feelings in my heart for all the times I listened to them on the freeways and boulevards of L.A.

I drove tens of thousands of miles to Eagles' songs on the 405, the 10, the 605, and the 110 freeways during flat outs and bumper-to-bumper backups. They accompanied me on PCH beach trips and during hauls to Berkeley and San Francisco. It was Eagles I listened to driving the I-5 grapevine when all I could see were thick dollops of fog and big rigs shrouded in the mist.

Eagles provided hope during our nation's most troubled times and that's no exaggeration: they saw us through Vietnam, Watergate, double-digit inflation, the gas crisis, hostages in Iran, and the Cold War. I'm talking about times when the nation was saddled by doubt and when cynicism and anger were on everyone's mind.

Thank you, guys, for "Lyin' Eyes," "Take It Easy," "Tequila Sunrise," "Life In the Fast Lane," "Best of My Love," "Already Gone," "Desperado," "Peaceful Easy Feeling," "Hotel California," "Victim Of Love," "I Can't Tell You Why," "Heartache Tonight," "Witchy Woman," "The Long Run," "Those Shoes," "Take It to the Limit," "New Kid in Town," and "One Of These Nights."

My girlfriend's out of the shower now, toweling off, long dark locks wet against her skin. "Good morning, baby," she says. I scroll through some more tweets about Frey and suddenly realize that I'm the dumb shit. I'm the asshole. It's too late to thank Glenn Frey because I finally realize what's happened. Henley's tweet isn't a tribute to his band mate, it's a heartfelt goodbye. Because Glenn Frey is dead. *Holy shit. Glenn Frey is dead.*

· · ·

I'VE BEEN HURTING SINCE FREY'S death a week ago and I can see my pain more clearly if I put on my Southern California lenses. Music means something different to us born in L.A. and it's because of our cars.

L.A. natives spend more time in their cars than any city in the nation. My family, friends and I were stuck in our cars every day because we had to go to work or school, get to the grocery store, visit our friends' houses, and get back home.

Those of us over forty remember radio as our companion during our time in L.A. because there was no other choice. FM radio soothed us at stoplights on Sunset and Barrington and while driving along Pico and Little Santa Monica Boulevard. Music wasn't just important to us Angelenos, it was the background to every car trip like the soundtrack to a movie.

Cars also gave us personas to inhabit if we had the ego and the money to blow. Wanna-be L.A. musician or surfer? Volkswagen bus or convertible. Producer? Old Porsche or Mercedes. Writer or Director? Vintage Oldsmobile or Cadillac. Cars were our refuge and our escape and the only place we were alone with our tunes. These were the days before CD players, MP3s, iTunes, Uber, Waze, Google Maps, podcasts, and satellite radio. It was the radio and the hits the DJ's played or nothing at all.

The rockers in L.A. listened to KLOS and KMET while alternative or new-wave music was played on KROQ. These FM stations meant everything to us because we self-identified our musical taste as soon as we matriculated to middle school. You announced your favorite radio station to your friends and it was like a gauntlet had been thrown down. *This is the music I like. Gotta problem with it?*

These radio stations played L.A. bands or bands we hoped were from L.A. so we could call them our own. Bands like Eagles, Tom Petty and the Heartbreakers, The Doors, Van Halen, David Bowie, The Motels, Missing Persons, Steely Dan, Mötley Crüe, and Fleetwood Mac.

Talk to an Angeleno and they'll tell you about DJs like Bob Coburn, Jim Ladd, Joe Benson, and Fraser Smith. We tuned in to them in the mornings and evenings during our two-and-a-half hour commutes because we loved their voices and considered them friends. They babysat us while our exhaust pipes pumped carbon monoxide onto the San Diego freeway, or when we thought we could skip the traffic altogether and take Sepulveda instead.

But still.

Glenn

Frey

is

dead.

I was floating in my favorite dream above the earth then woke up to reality and wished I hadn't. Glenn Frey was still dead and it was one of the saddest days of my life.

I mean, it was only last week that David Bowie had died. Bowie! And I was at work when I heard that news, and I was like Bowie? Bowie! And hardly anyone at work even knows who Frey or Bowie are because they're recent college graduates and I'm as old as a castle.

I mean, even *I'm* too young to know Bowie because he was a bit before my time, but I knew enough of his hits to know that he was an artist. A multi-talented actor, musician, lyricist, songwriter, fashionista, trendsetter, and painter, and not a product spit out by some Century City suits brainstorming over low fat muffins and cold-pressed juice. And now that Bowie's gone, too, all I want to do is hear him play to take away the pain.

And then I'm scanning my news feed and learn that Alan Rickman has died. Alan Rickman is dead? 'Hans' from *Die Hard* is gone? I'm absolutely devastated at this trifecta of artistic losses and try to compose myself. Rickman's talents were imprinted on my soul because he personified one of the most believable screen villains of the modern era: Hans Gruber from *Die Hard*. And now he's dead. Hans is dead.

It's not just Rickman's death that hurts, but that social media is thrumming with the news that 'Snape' from the Harry Potter movies has died. Snape? Snape! Are you kidding me? I'm in a well of grief over here and you're recognizing Rickman for Harry Potter? Are you out of your fucking mind?

The news that Rickman has shuffled off this mortal coil arrives to me when I'm at work so I look around desperately for a contemporary with whom I can commiserate about this horrific loss but there's no one. *Die Hard* isn't exactly in the wheelhouse of my coworkers because classic action films aren't big on my team. I grieve alone on the day that the greatest movie villain in history dies and I wonder if anyone even remembers John McClane yelling the movie's catchphrase: *yippee-ki-yay!*

So there I am at my desk and I have to cope with the deaths of Bowie, Rickman, and Frey and I just slump my head in my hands and close my eyes.

Rickman's American accent in the rooftop scene from *Die Hard* was unforgettable and I'm desperate to talk to someone about it. Whom can I talk to at work to relive one of the best scenes in his greatest role? Let me share it with you now and set the stage.

John McClane (Willis) and Hans Gruber (Rickman) end up alone on the rooftop of the Nakatomi Plaza building in Act II. I'm not sure if you remember the building, but it's key to the plot and where the action unfolds in downtown Los Angeles (the real life building was the Fox Plaza in Century City). The rooftop scene is crucial because McClane has been in a pitched battle with the terrorists in a wicked game of cat and mouse and he mistakes Hans for a hostage and not the wily terrorist that he is. And it's all due to British actor Rickman's masterful American accent.

You've got to hand it to the filmmakers on this one because this is how cool collaborative art can be. It was Rickman's casual imitation of the American dialect that inspired the film's screenwriters to write the scene.

Steven E. de Souza and Jeb Stuart penned this masterpiece of a script and they and the entire production team deserve our heartfelt thanks for such a great film. I wonder if anyone even knows the writers who penned the lines from their favorite films. "Your move, chief" wasn't written by Robin Williams for "Good Will Hunting." It was written by Matt Damon and Ben Affleck. "I am your father," spoken by Darth Vader in "Empire Strikes Back" was a line of dialogue from a combined script penned by Leigh Brackett, Lawrence Kasdan, and George Lucas. All of the work was collaborative.

The actors in *Die Hard* were part of an enormous ensemble of artists who brought the film to fruition through hard work and a fair amount of good luck. So while I weep for Frey and Bowie and Rickman, I also weep for the serendipity that brings us great art.

I grieve for the interplay of creativity, where the sum is greater than the parts and where amazing art changes us all. I think it's rare to find this creative interplay on earth and we should celebrate it from the mountaintops when we find it because it brings meaning to our lives.

But now I'm done grieving and I'm ready to move on. I've said my thanks to my heroes and can't do much more. So here's to you all and thanks for everything. I just fucking miss you guys.

*Don Henley and Eagles have spoken extensively about Glenn Frey since Frey's death. Any suggestion that Eagles were insensitive or disrespectful to Frey on social media is unintentional. They weren't. See Eagles' web site for more thoughts on Glenn Frey at www.eagles.com.

ABOUT BRIAN BARTON

I always wanted to write. I wrote when I was younger to express myself and I do the same thing today. I'm a big reader, too. Books, magazines, cereal boxes. Anything. Every project starts with research because I like to learn about a subject before I begin. I read, travel, and interview people and take notes on what I learn. I immerse myself in a topic because it's interesting and then start writing. This can take anywhere from months to years. When I'm done, I work with professional artists to create book designs that I hope will capture your imagination. The result is writing steeped in real life. I hope you enjoy it.

ACKNOWLEDGMENTS

Thanks to D.M.T., Emily, J.Y, Julia, and Ronit.

THANK YOU

Thanks for your emails, tweets, comments, and questions. Word of mouth is essential for self-published authors like me. Please write a review on Amazon or Goodreads if you can. Thanks.

—*B.B.*
New York City

www.ingramcontent.com/pod-product-compliance
Lightning Source LLC
Chambersburg PA
CBHW070844310526
45793CB00011B/527